Music Genres

Jazz

by Trudy Becker

FOCUS READERS®
BEACON

www.focusreaders.com

Focus Readers is distributed by North Star Editions:
sales@northstareditions.com | 888-417-0195

Produced for Focus Readers by Red Line Editorial.

Photographs ©: Chris Pizzello/Invision/AP Images, cover, 1; Shutterstock Images, 4, 6, 8, 14, 22, 25, 26; iStockphoto, 11, 12, 29; Michael Ochs Archives/Getty Images, 17; Bob Wands/AP Images, 19; Roland Witschel/picture-alliance/dpa/AP Images, 20–21

Library of Congress Cataloging-in-Publication Data
Names: Becker, Trudy, author.
Title: Jazz / by Trudy Becker.
Description: Mendota Heights, MN: Focus Readers, 2025. | Series: Music genres | Includes index. | Audience: Grades 2-3
Identifiers: LCCN 2024001543 (print) | LCCN 2024001544 (ebook) | ISBN 9798889982012 (hardcover) | ISBN 9798889982579 (paperback) | ISBN 9798889983651 (pdf) | ISBN 9798889983132 (ebook)
Subjects: LCSH: Jazz--History and criticism--Juvenile literature.
Classification: LCC ML3506 .B4307 2025 (print) | LCC ML3506 (ebook) | DDC 781.6509--dc23/eng/20240112
LC record available at https://lccn.loc.gov/2024001543
LC ebook record available at https://lccn.loc.gov/2024001544

Printed in the United States of America
Mankato, MN
082024

About the Author

Trudy Becker lives in Minneapolis, Minnesota. She loves listening to many genres of music.

Table of Contents

Green Mill

Chapter 1

Playing Jazz

The lights are dim in the jazz club. People lounge in soft chairs. A performance is about to begin. The audience is excited. All eyes look toward the small stage.

One of the oldest jazz clubs in the United States is the Green Mill in Chicago, Illinois.

Many jazz clubs have performances from local musicians.

Several musicians step onto the stage. They are tonight's jazz band. The first player sits down at a piano. Another waits at a drum set. Others hold trumpets and saxophones. Then the leader gives a signal. The band starts playing.

The music moves with a swinging beat. A spotlight shifts between players. Each plays a solo. The jazz fans smile. They bop their heads to the **rhythm**.

Many of the first jazz clubs in the United States were in New Orleans, Louisiana.

Chapter 2

What Is Jazz Music?

Jazz is a type of music from the southeastern United States. The music comes from a mix of sources. So, jazz includes many sounds. But the **genre** has a few common features.

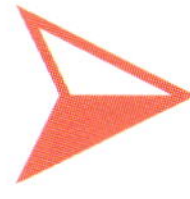

Early jazz guitars were acoustic. In modern times, musicians often use electric guitars.

Jazz music often uses drums, bass, guitar, and keyboard. A singer might perform the song's main tune. Or an instrument might play it. Trumpet, trombone, and saxophone are common choices.

Rhythm is one of the most important parts of jazz. Jazz often includes **syncopated** rhythms. Notes come on **offbeats**. That can give the music a groove. Jazz often uses "swung" rhythms, too. Swung notes come in pairs. The first note

Many kinds of swing dances are done to jazz music.

is longer. The second is short. Together, these notes give the music a swaying feeling. Many jazz rhythms are simpler versions of old West African rhythms.

Musicians can bend notes on instruments such as trumpets. They can bend notes while singing, too.

Jazz uses many types of **harmony** and chords. Some sound pleasing to people's ears. Other sounds are more **dissonant**. For example, jazz often uses "bent" or "blue" notes. Players shift the sound up or down. The notes sound a little higher or lower than usual. The shift helps the music show strong feelings.

Improvisation is important in jazz, too. Jazz players often improvise during solos. That gives their performances freedom and looseness. The same song sounds different each time it is played.

In many jazz bands, each instrument has a role. For example, the clarinet often supports the main **melody**.

Chapter 3

Jazz Music History

In the early 1800s, people gathered in Congo Square. The square was in New Orleans, Louisiana. On weekends, enslaved people danced and played music there. Some free people joined.

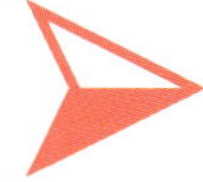

A sculpture in New Orleans shows people dancing in Congo Square.

Many of these people had African, Caribbean, and European roots.

Over time, more music genres added to the mix of sounds. People played ragtime. They played blues. Brass instruments from military marching bands also had influence. All those sounds came together. They grew into New Orleans jazz music.

Most of these early jazz sounds came from Black musicians. But the first jazz recordings came from

Cornet player Bix Beiderbecke (right) was a famous early jazz musician.

white artists. That was because of racism in the music industry. Companies didn't want to promote Black artists. So, those artists did not get credit. Still, the genre began to grow.

The 1920s were called the Roaring Twenties. Jazz music hit a high point. Duke Ellington played in New York jazz clubs. Count Basie started a famous jazz band. Louis Armstrong became a huge star.

Later, other genres replaced jazz at the top of the charts. But jazz singers such as Ella Fitzgerald and

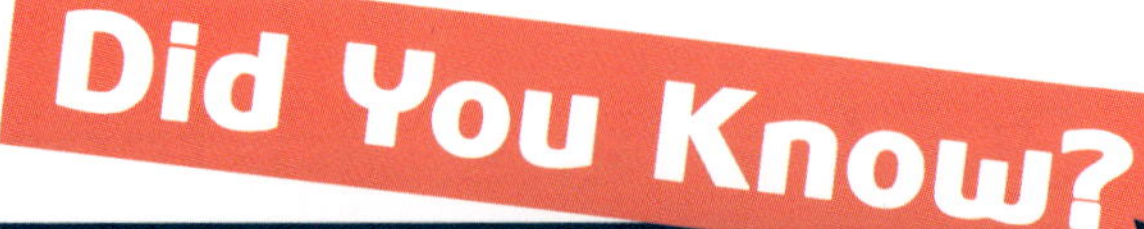

Jazz is sometimes called "America's classical music."

Duke Ellington (left) and Louis Armstrong (right) recorded music together later in their careers.

Nina Simone still moved listeners. And subgenres such as modern jazz and free jazz developed.

ARTIST SPOTLIGHT

Louis Armstrong

Louis Armstrong was born in New Orleans in 1901. When he was young, he learned to play **cornet**. He dreamed of being a musician. So, he went to Chicago, Illinois. He joined the famous band of Joseph "King" Oliver.

Over the years, Armstrong performed amazing cornet and trumpet solos. He was a singer, too. His emotional voice attracted many listeners. Armstrong became the first superstar of jazz. His music influenced the genre for many decades.

Many people consider Louis Armstrong one of the best trumpeters in history.

Blue Note
JAZZ
CAPITAL OF THE WORLD
Blue Note
Blue Note
らーめん屋
Beyond

Chapter 4

Jazz Today

Over time, jazz became less mainstream. Its radio play and sales went down. But jazz never went away. By the end of the 1900s, it was still a thriving genre. Listeners loved visiting jazz clubs.

In the early 2020s, New York City had more jazz clubs than any other city in the world.

Many were active across the United States. Global cities such as Paris, France, and Cape Town, South Africa, had major jazz scenes, too.

In the 1980s and 1990s, smooth jazz was a popular subgenre. Smooth jazz is calm and soft. It is made for easy listening. Artists also mixed jazz with more and more genres. They combined jazz with funk, rock, pop, and R&B.

By the 2010s and 2020s, new stars began emerging. Singers

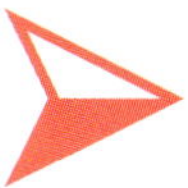

In the 1980s and 1990s, Anita Baker sang smooth jazz hits. She also sang R&B and other genres.

such as Cécile McLorin Salvant delighted listeners. So did trumpeter Brandon Woody. Many younger artists helped move the genre forward. These artists blended old and new styles.

Samara Joy released her first album in 2021.

For example, a group called Ezra Collective mixed jazz with hip-hop. Young people also learned jazz in school. High school students played in thousands of jazz bands across the United States. Jazz festivals were held around the world.

Each year, the Grammys give an award for Best New Artist. In 2023, the winner was Samara Joy. She was a rising jazz artist. Through Joy and many other new artists, the future of jazz was in good hands.

At first, jazz music was mostly played for dancing. Later, audiences mostly sat and listened.

FOCUS ON

Jazz

Write your answers on a separate piece of paper.

1. Write a few sentences explaining common features of jazz music.

2. Would you want to be part of a jazz band? Why or why not?

3. When was the high point for jazz?

- **A.** 1820s
- **B.** 1920s
- **C.** 1980s

4. How could mixing jazz with other styles help jazz reach more listeners?

- **A.** People might start liking other genres instead of jazz.
- **B.** People who liked other styles might start liking jazz, too.
- **C.** People always think jazz sounds better without mixing genres.

5. What does **mainstream** mean in this book?

Over time, jazz became less ***mainstream****. Its radio play and sales went down.*

A. popular
B. secret
C. difficult

6. What does **thriving** mean in this book?

By the end of the 1900s, it was still a ***thriving*** *genre. Listeners loved visiting jazz clubs. Many were active across the United States.*

A. no longer played
B. played in few places
C. doing well

Answer key on page 32.

Glossary

cornet
A brass instrument that is similar to a trumpet.

dissonant
Blending sounds in a way that clashes or feels tense.

genre
A category of music, such as rock, pop, or country.

harmony
The blending of notes played or sung together.

improvisation
The act of playing music without planning the notes, rhythms, and melodies ahead of time.

melody
The tune in a piece of music.

offbeats
The beats that are often weaker or less emphasized in a piece of music.

rhythm
In music, the mix of short and long sounds that create patterns.

syncopated
When strong notes are not on the main beats.

To Learn More

BOOKS

Abdo, Kenny. *Jazz Music History*. Minneapolis: Abdo Publishing, 2020.

Powell, Chyina. *Duke Ellington*. Mendota Heights, MN: Focus Readers, 2023.

Sommer, Nathan. *Louisiana*. Minneapolis: Bellwether Media, 2022.

NOTE TO EDUCATORS

Visit **www.focusreaders.com** to find lesson plans, activities, links, and other resources related to this title.

Index

Answer Key: 1. Answers will vary; **2.** Answers will vary; **3.** B; **4.** B; **5.** A; **6.** C